P9-DCV-043

TRAVEL WITH THE GREAT EXPLORERS

Explore with

Ponce de León

Cynthia O'Brien

Crabtree Publishing Company
www.crabtreebooks.com

Crabtree Publishing Company
www.crabtreebooks.com

Author: Cynthia O'Brien
**Publishing plan research
and development:** Reagan Miller
Managing Editor: Tim Cooke
Editors: Crystal Sikkens, Shannon Welbourn
Designer: Lynne Lennon
Picture Manager: Sophie Mortimer
Design Manager: Keith Davis
Editorial Director: Lindsey Lowe
Children's Publisher: Anne O'Daly
**Production coordinator
and prepress technician:** Tammy McGarr
Print coordinator: Katherine Berti

Produced by Brown Bear Books for
Crabtree Publishing Company

Photographs:
Front Cover: Shutterstock: Carlos Caetano tr, Eric Isselée br,
Daniel Korzeniewski cr; Topfoto: The Granger Collection main.

Interior: Alamy: Mary Evans Picture Library 4, Melvyn Longhurst
18, North Wind Picture Archives 27l, Pictorial Press Ltd 21b, The Art
Gallery Collection 25t; Getty Images: DeAgostini 19; Mary Evans
Picture Library: 26; Public Domain: 11b, Gemaldegalerie, Berin 7b,
Alexandrew de Batz 21b; Robert Hunt Library: 13b, 16bl, 20t, 27r,
28b; Shutterstock: 12, 17t, 25b, Songquan Deng 5b Borya Galperin
21b, Hurst Photo 15r, Peter Kratochvil 21t, Peter Leahy 22,
Don Mammoser 6, Photo Fun 17b; Thinkstock: Hemera 11t,
istockphoto 14, 23, 28t, 29, Photos.com 5t, 10t, 13t, 15l, 16t,
Stockbyte 10-11t; Topfoto: The Granger Collection 24.

All other artwork and maps © Brown Bear Books Ltd.

Brown Bear Books has made every attempt to contact the
copyright holder. If you have any information please contact
licensing@brownbearbooks.co.uk

Library and Archives Canada Cataloguing in Publication

O'Brien, Cynthia (Cynthia J.), author
    Explore with Ponce de León / Cynthia O'Brien.

(Travel with the great explorers)
Includes index.
Issued in print and electronic formats.
ISBN 978-0-7787-1429-3 (bound).--ISBN 978-0-7787-1435-4 (pbk.).--
ISBN 978-1-4271-7590-8 (pdf).--ISBN 978-1-4271-7580-9 (html)

    1. Ponce de León, Juan, 1460?-1521--Juvenile literature.
2. Explorers--Spain--Biography--Juvenile literature. 3. Explorers--
America--Biography--Juvenile literature. 4. America--Discovery
and exploration--Spanish--Juvenile literature. I. Title.

E125.P7O37 2014   j910'.92   C2014-903750-3
                                           C2014-903751-1

Library of Congress Cataloging-in-Publication Data

O'Brien, Cynthia (Cynthia J.)
  Explore with Ponce de León / Cynthia O'Brien.
    pages cm. -- (Travel with the great explorers)
  Includes index.
  ISBN 978-0-7787-1429-3 (reinforced library binding) --
ISBN 978-0-7787-1435-4 (pbk.) -- ISBN 978-1-4271-7590-8 (electronic
pdf) -- ISBN 978-1-4271-7580-9 (electronic html)
  1. Ponce de León, Juan, 1460?-1521--Juvenile literature. 2.
Explorers--America--Biography--Juvenile literature. 3. Explorers-
-Spain--Biography--Juvenile literature. 4. Florida--Discovery and
exploration--Spanish--Juvenile literature. 5. America--Discovery
and exploration--Spanish--Juvenile literature. I. Title.

E125.P7O27 2015
910.92--dc23
[B]
                                           2014020966

Crabtree Publishing Company

www.crabtreebooks.com   1-800-387-7650

Printed in Hong Kong/082014/BK20140613

Published in Canada
Crabtree Publishing
616 Welland Ave.
St. Catharines, ON
L2M 5V6

Published in the United States
Crabtree Publishing
PMB 59051
350 Fifth Avenue, 59th Floor
New York, New York 10118

Published in the United Kingdom
Crabtree Publishing
Maritime House
Basin Road North, Hove
BN41 1WR

Published in Australia
Crabtree Publishing
3 Charles Street
Coburg North
VIC, 3058

CONTENTS

Meet the Boss

The young Spaniard Juan Ponce de León hoped the New World would bring him glory and a chance for fortune. He explored the Caribbean as well as a land he named Florida.

AMERICA!

Spanish exploration of the New World began in 1492. Christopher Columbus landed on Hispaniola, now the Dominican Republic.

THE YOUNG PAGE

☛ **Learning the ropes**

☛ **Rising through the ranks**

Ponce de León was born in northwestern Spain sometime between 1460 and 1474. As a young boy, he acted as a **page** for a Spanish knight. Ponce de León later learned to ride a horse and handle weapons. As a **squire**, he joined military campaigns. By his late teens, he was a trained and experienced soldier.

CHRISTIAN SOLDIER

+ **Squire fights in historic battle**

+ **Spanish take Granada**

The Moors were **Muslims** from North Africa. They occupied much of southern Spain and fought Spanish Christians for hundreds of years for control of the land. In 1487, Ponce de León joined the fight to capture the last Moorish-held fortress in Spain—Granada. In 1492, the Christians finally defeated the Moors at Granada and drove them from Spain.

QUEST FOR ADVENTURE

★ Rulers sponsor explorations

In the late 1400s, the Spanish rulers—King Ferdinand and Queen Isabella—wanted to spread the Catholic faith and claim land for Spain. Spanish explorers sailed across the oceans in the name of the crown. In 1493, Christopher Columbus embarked on his second voyage to the New World for Spain. It is possible that the young Juan Ponce de León accompanied him. However, Columbus's trip was a failure, so Ponce de León returned to the Caribbean to lead his own expeditions.

THE ENFORCER

+ Governor sends troops to fight Taíno

No one is sure what Ponce de León did after his first voyage to America in 1493. But he crossed the Atlantic again in 1502. Nicolás Ovando was **governor** of the Spanish **colony** on the island of Hispaniola in the Caribbean. He struggled to control the Taíno, the native people who still controlled part of the island. In 1504, Ponce de León joined the Spanish forces to attack the Taíno. He helped defeat them and received land and money for his efforts. Ponce de León was on his way to fame and fortune.

> **"Discoverer and first governor of Florida: valiant military man, skillful leader, loyal subject."**
> *Words on Ponce de León's tomb*

Where Are We Heading?

Ponce de León settled on the island of Hispaniola. He established farms, became governor, and set off for a land the local Taíno called Bimini.

SPANISH SETTLEMENT

★ **Spain takes over Hispaniola**

By the time Ponce de León arrived on Hispaniola in 1504, the Spanish colony was flourishing. He received an **encomienda** for his efforts in the battle against the Taíno and became governor of the province of Hugüey. For four years, the Spanish soldier was a successful landowner and farmer.

ISLAND GOLD

☛ **Royal permission granted**

☛ **Ponce de León founds settlement**

In 1508, the Spanish king allowed Ponce de León to make an expedition to San Juan Bautista. The explorer landed in a bay he called Puerto Rico, meaning "rich port." Ponce de León established a colony near the bay and became governor. This part of the island became known as Puerto Rico. He was replaced by Diego Columbus two years later, so Ponce de León decided to set his sights elsewhere.

THE PLACE OF FLOWERS

★ **Taíno described rich land to the north**

★ **Ponce de León sets out to explore**

After losing his position as governor of Puerto Rico, Ponce de León made a decision. He decided to search for an island the Taíno had told him about called Bimini. On March 27, 1513, the explorer spotted land that he believed was an island. He landed on the eastern coast on April 2, 1513. It was Easter, and Ponce de León named the land, La Florida, after *Pascua de Florida*, the Spanish name for the holiday which means "feast of flowers".,

THE SEARCH FOR ETERNAL YOUTH

☛ **Does the fountain exist?**

One famous story spoke of Ponce de León going to Florida to try to find a fountain he had heard about. It was believed the fountain had magical water, keeping anyone who drank from it eternally young. The story was recorded 10 years after Ponce de León's death by a writer called Oviedo, who did not like Ponce de León. There is no other record that Ponce de León believed the fountain existed.

RIDING THE GULF STREAM

+ **A quick crossing**

Sailing near Florida in 1513, Ponce de León noted, "the current was more powerful than the wind." He and his **pilot**, Antón de Alaminos, had found the Gulf Stream. This current flows from the Gulf of Mexico across the Atlantic Ocean. It made sailing to Europe quicker.

Ponce de León's Voyage to Florida

NORTH AMERICA

Ponce de León had already discovered and settled Puerto Rico when he set off in 1513 to look for a land to the north called Bimini. At Easter, he found what he thought was a large island and named it Florida.

Gulf of Mexico

Mexico

Charlotte Harbor

It was probably near Charlotte Harbor that Ponce de León first encountered the Calusa, who attacked his ships in war canoes. On his return to Florida in 1521, he was fatally wounded by a Calusa arrow and died later.

Las Tortugas

Sailing southwest in 1513 from Florida, Ponce de León discovered an island rich in turtles (*tortugas* in Spanish) and seabirds. His men killed many animals for food. Today, the island is known as Dry Tortuga, as it has no fresh water.

Havana

After Ponce de León was wounded in a fight with the Calusa in June or July 1521, his crew sailed with him to the capital of Spanish-owned Cuba. Ponce de León's wound became infected, and he died there in July 1521.

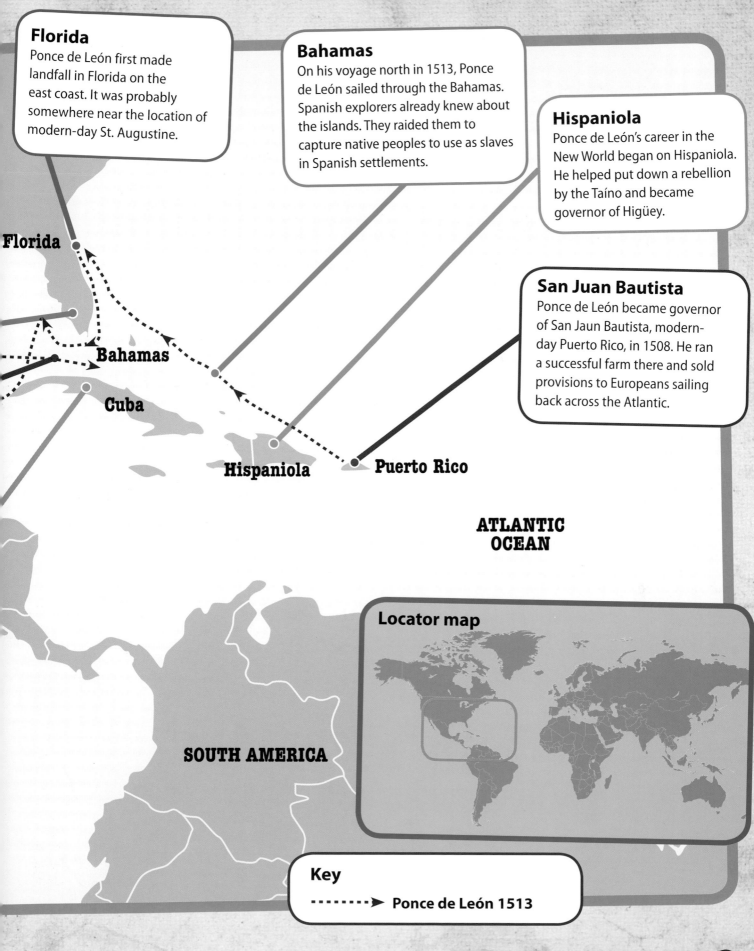

Florida
Ponce de León first made landfall in Florida on the east coast. It was probably somewhere near the location of modern-day St. Augustine.

Bahamas
On his voyage north in 1513, Ponce de León sailed through the Bahamas. Spanish explorers already knew about the islands. They raided them to capture native peoples to use as slaves in Spanish settlements.

Hispaniola
Ponce de León's career in the New World began on Hispaniola. He helped put down a rebellion by the Taíno and became governor of Higüey.

San Juan Bautista
Ponce de León became governor of San Jaun Bautista, modern-day Puerto Rico, in 1508. He ran a successful farm there and sold provisions to Europeans sailing back across the Atlantic.

Florida

Bahamas

Cuba

Hispaniola

Puerto Rico

ATLANTIC OCEAN

Locator map

SOUTH AMERICA

Key
------▶ **Ponce de León 1513**

Meet the Crew

Knights, kings, and other nobles recognized and supported Ponce de León's skills and ambitions. Others tried to take away his power and ruin his name.

Did you know?

King Ferdinand and Queen Isabella completed the reconquest of Spain. In 1492, they defeated the last Moorish kingdom.

THE CATHOLIC CONNECTION

☞ **Royal backing for New World exploration**

Spain's "Catholic Monarchs," King Ferdinand and Queen Isabella, were powerful rulers. After banishing the Moors from Spain, they reunited the country under their Christian rule. The king and queen then turned their attention to exploration. By law, explorers needed the crown's permission to launch expeditions. Ponce de León asked for approval for each voyage. Many others did not and sailed without permission.

I THINK I'VE BEEN REPLACED

★ **Diego Columbus claims Puerto Rico**

King Ferdinand granted the governorship of Puerto Rico to Ponce de León. However, Christopher Columbus's son, Diego, went to court to claim the island based on the fact that his father had discovered it first. After some back and forth in 1511, Diego won, and Ponce de León decided to step down.

HUMBLE BEGINNINGS

+ Learning on the job

Antón de Alaminos began his career as a cabin boy for Christopher Columbus and became a skilled sailor. He settled in Hispaniola and then in Cuba. De Alaminos was the pilot for Ponce's voyage to Florida. Years later, he was the pilot for Francisco Hernández de Córdoba on his trip to the Yucatan Peninsula. He also piloted for Hernán Cortés on his expedition to Mexico.

BESTSELLING AUTHOR

+ Royal historian

Gonzalo Fernandez de Oviedo y Valdes was the official historian for the Spanish crown. Oviedo visited the New World for the first time in 1514 and returned several times. In 1535, he became famous for his book *General and Natural History of the Indies* (right). It told the story of Spanish exploration.

A NEW ORDER

★ **Charles V crowned king of Spain**

★ **Ponce seeks approval for new journey**

After Ponce de León had claimed Florida for Spain, he headed across the Atlantic to speak with the king. While he was there, the recently crowned King Charles V awarded the explorer rights to explore the new land. The king also named Ponce de León governor of Bimini (Florida).

Check Out the Ride

Europeans needed large, sturdy vessels to cross the Atlantic Ocean. In the New World, smaller ships were useful for exploring shallow waters around islands and coasts.

Did you know?

At the time of Ponce de León's voyages, Spain led the world in shipbuilding. It had created new vessels for crossing the oceans.

RIDING THE WAVES

- Caravels favored for speed
- Suited to high seas

The *Santiago*, a **caravel**, was one of three ships in Ponce de León's fleet. This swift ship was ideally suited to making long journeys. Its high sides meant it could withstand powerful ocean waves. However, it was also small enough to explore near coasts and smaller waterways. The *Santiago* carried a small crew to explore the island of Bimini.

SANTA MARIÁ DE LA CONSOLACIÓN

★ Flagship sets sail for Bimini

A large ship, called a carrack, carried Ponce de León north. The carrack was a transport ship. Explorers used it to carry people and goods on longer journeys. Its main deck was large enough to fit the crew and cannons. The deep hull, or body, of the ship had lots of room for cargo.

TRAVEL UPDATE

Sea Monsters!

★ Sailors could become worried and tense by stories about sea monsters in the Atlantic. But as more sailors were visiting the New World safely, it seemed that the stories may have been exaggerated. However, sailors still kept a look out.

Juana

Juana Ruiz was one of the passengers on Ponce de León's ship, *Santa Mariá de la Consolación*. She was the first European woman to set foot in Florida.

TURNING TREES INTO BOATS

+ Dugouts popular transport in the Gulf

The Taíno and other Caribbean native peoples made dugout canoes. These were boats made by hollowing out trees. The Taíno used ceiba trees. The Calusa used cypress logs and carved canoes about 15 feet (4.5 meters) long. They traveled as far as Cuba to trade. Some dugout canoes could carry up to 80 people. Several people used paddles to move the canoes through the water.

Solve It With Science

Follow Me

On board a ship, the responsibility for steering a course belonged to the pilot. A pilot was skilled in using maps and navigational devices.

Ponce de León was a soldier, not a sailor. He relied on experienced navigators to guide his ships. His ships carried both instruments for navigation and the latest weapons.

CALCULATE THIS!

☛ Dead reckoning determines location

Skilled navigators found their location at sea by **dead reckoning**. This system used a calculation of the ship's speed and the time traveled since the previous reading. Dead reckoning was not precise, but it provided useful information. This was especially true when the skies were cloudy, and navigators could not see the stars they usually steered by.

POINTING THE WAY

+ Compass pinpoints direction

The Chinese invented the **compass** in the 3rd century BCE. By the 15th century, all explorers used the compass. The instrument uses a **magnetized** needle than spins around so that it always points north. A compass did not depend on sunlight, stars, or good weather to work.

Did you know?

In the 15th century navigators were good at finding out how far north or south they were—but not how far east or west.

NORTH OR SOUTH?

☛ **Heavy-metal masters**

Latitude is the distance north or south of the equator. It is measured in degrees. The **equator** is at 0° (degrees). Navigators used a **cross-staff** or **quadrant** to calculate latitude. These instruments measured the height of a star or the sun above the horizon. Ponce de León landed in Florida at 30° 8′ north, near present-day St. Augustine.

My Explorer Journal

★ Imagine that you are one of the Calusa people. You have never seen firearms before. How do you think you would react to the Spanish arquebuses?

TRAVEL UPDATE

Sand Tracks the Minutes

★ Sand timers were good for keeping track of time. With two glass bulbs connected by a thin tube, sand flowed from one bulb to the other. A cabin boy would turn the timer each time all the sand had fallen into the bottom bulb, which was 30 minutes. At each turn, he rang a bell so sailors could measure their turns on watch.

GUNS VS. ARROWS

★ **Spanish surprise Calusa with firearms**

★ **Europeans have the advantage**

Ponce de León's crew carried long rifles, called **arquebuses**, on his first expedition to Florida. Each night, his ships anchored near the coast. When the Spaniards went ashore, the Calusa attacked them with arrows, injuring some of the crew. The Spanish fired their arquebuses, frightening the Calusa away.

Hanging at Home

Although Ponce de León and other wealthy Spaniards lived quite comfortably, others did not fare so well. Sailors endured difficult sea voyages, and settlers faced attacks by the islanders.

ROUGHING IT

+ **Life aboard ship**

+ **Surviving the trip**

In Ponce de León's time, journeys across the ocean meant hard work. Sailors often slept on deck or in small cots. They ate salted meat and fish and dry biscuits, and drank wine. Fresh vegetables and fruit ran out quickly on long trips. Without fresh food, many sailors died of **scurvy**.

LIFE ON THE FARM

★ **Ponce de León awarded encomienda**

★ **Governor marries**

After receiving a land grant on Hispaniola, Ponce de León began farming. A successful businessman, Ponce de León sold his produce to traders to take back to Spain. In 1502, he married an innkeeper's daughter, Leonora, a Spanish woman he had met on the island. The couple had four children.

YOU LOOK A LITTLE GREEN!

- Oviedo criticizes Caparra
- Swamp possible cause of illness

In Puerto Rico, Ponce de León built a settlement named Caparra on high ground near a protected bay. The settlement was successful for a time, but Oviedo noted that the settlers turned a little green because Ponce de León had foolishly built the colony next to a swamp. In 1519, the king ordered the settlers to move the colony to San Juan Bay.

PARADISE FOUND AND LOST

★ Spaniards attacked

King Ferdinand awarded Ponce de León the right to settle Florida. Eight years after his first trip, Ponce de León set out to found a colony. In February 1521, he took 200 settlers to Florida. Shortly after landing, the Calusa attacked and forced the Spanish to withdraw to Cuba. They settled in what is now Havana. Ponce de León did not live to see Florida colonized.

Did you know?

The settlement at Caparra was never reoccupied after it was abandoned. Today, only a few ruins mark the site.

Meeting and Greeting

The Spanish held tightly onto control of their territory in the Americas, which led to revolt and conflict with the native peoples. Slavery and disease took its toll on the Taíno people.

Weather Forecast

DRESSED FOR SUMMER

Europeans were often shocked to find that native peoples in the Caribbean and Florida wore few clothes. In fact, the hot summers and the short, mild winters meant that clothes were not really needed for warmth or protection.

GOOD AND NOBLE PEOPLE

- Taíno population disappears
- Spanish seek islanders' gold

When Ponce de León arrived in Puerto Rico in 1508, the Taíno lived among several villages in wooden houses with straw roofs. They wore jewelry that convinced the Spaniards that the island was rich in gold. They made the Taíno work in gold mines.

Did you know?

The Carib people were fierce rivals of the Taíno. Ponce de León said he would help protect the Taíno if the Taíno worked the land and mined for gold.

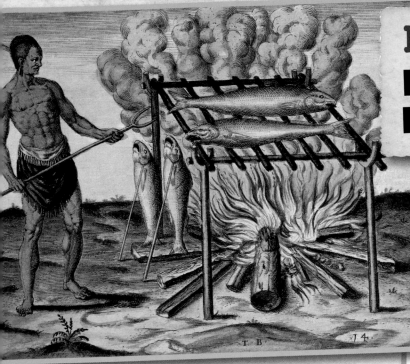

MOUND FARMING

+ **Spanish grew local food**

+ **Used system of mounds**

The Taíno understood the land and knew how to grow crops. They made rows in the ground from mounds of earth. The mounds, called *conuncos*, were about 3 feet (1 m) high. Here, the Taíno planted **yucca**, or cassava, sweet potatoes, and tobacco. Ponce de León used this same farming system to grow food on his encomienda.

SLAVE LABOR

★ **Taíno helped at Caparra**

★ **Spanish abused Taíno**

Ponce de León tried to treat the Taíno fairly, but as part of the encomienda system he was allowed to force them to work for him. He could also make the Taíno work for other settlers on farms or in mines. Conditions were hard. By 1520, only 1,000 Taíno survived.

TRICKS OF THE TRADE

☛ **Learning from the Taíno**

☛ **Locals point the way to other lands**

The Taíno taught the Spanish how to farm in the New World and introduced them to new crops such as tobacco. The Taíno also knew about the surrounding islands. Their tales led to Ponce de León's exploration of Florida and the surrounding area.

People of Florida

Ponce de León probably encountered the Tequesta people on his first trip to Florida. On his second trip, he met the Calusa warriors—and they were not very friendly.

WHO ARE YOU?

☛ **Florida's people**

Ponce de León first landed in eastern Florida. At that time, Florida was home to five different native tribes. The explorer may have encountered the Tequesta or the Timucua, both peaceful people. The Calusa lived on the southern and western coasts. They were fishers and hunters. They attacked Spaniards who tried to settle there. Oviedo described the Calusa as "ferocious."

SPANISH ATTACKED!

+ **Contact unsuccessful**

+ **Spanish attacked**

In 1513, Ponce de León met the Calusa as he explored Florida's Gulf Coast. He believed the Calusa were willing to trade gold, but Calusa warriors in 80 canoes rowed out to threaten the Spanish ship. The Calusa fired arrows at the ship, but the Spaniards scared them away with guns.

THE SHELL PEOPLE

★ **Uses for seashells**

★ **Shell mounds**

The Calusa used shells in their jewelry, as tools, and on their spears. They created mounds of shells and clay, called **middens**. Many middens still exist in southern Florida. **Archaeologists** believe that one of these sites, Mound Key at Estero Bay, Lee County, was the home of Chief Carlos, the Calusa leader.

UNDER THE PALMS

★ **Homes allowed the breeze in**

Florida is warm and sunny, so the Calusa did not need much shelter. They built their homes on stilts near the water's edge, so incoming tides could flow underneath. They made roofs from the leaves of the Palmetto plants that grew all around them.

My Explorer Journal

★ **The Taíno welcomed the Spanish, while the Calusa fought against them. How do you think you would have reacted to the newcomers? Provide your reasons.**

Poison!

Native peoples used different poisons on their arrows. The Taíno made poison from arrowroot. The Calusa used the sap of the manchineel tree.

DEADLY WEAPONS

☞ **Calusa arrows laced with poison?**

The Calusa used shells to make tips for their arrows. Many native peoples put poison on arrow tips. When the Spaniards fought the Calusa in 1521, Ponce de Léon was hit by a poison arrow. He later died of the infected wound.

I Love Nature

The New World presented a wide range of plants and animals for the Spanish to discover. They sent stories of new creatues and many new foods back to Spain.

Mmm...

Iguana meat was widely eaten in parts of Mexico and Central America. Today, iguanas are a threatened species, and it is illegal to hunt them in many countries.

TURTLE ISLANDS

☛ **Nesting reptiles startled Spanish**

After exploring Florida's coastline, Ponce de León sailed southwest past an island where sea turtles were nesting. He named the island Las Tortugas. In a single night, Ponce de León's men captured and killed 160 turtles.

BREAD OF LIFE

+ Yucca plant provided food for many

+ Ponce de León sees profit in local plant

The islanders grew a variety of foods, but yucca, or cassava, was their main crop. The plant was poisonous if eaten raw, but the Taíno cooked it in bread and in soups and stews. Ponce de León planted cassava on his farm. He made bread to sell to the Spanish in the colony and to people sailing back to Europe. It stayed fresh a long time making it ideal for ocean voyages.

TRY IT! YOU'LL LIKE IT!

★ **Lizard delicacy**

★ **Fit for a king**

The Taíno hunted small animals on Puerto Rico but only chiefs were allowed to eat iguanas. The Spaniards did not like the idea of eating a reptile, but Oviedo wrote that it tasted, "as good or better than rabbit."

My Explorer Journal

★ **Using the picture on this page, write a description of an iguana for someone who has never seen one.**

OH SO SWEET!

☛ **Spanish add new foods to their diet**

☛ **Taíno menu**

The Spanish discovered delicious foods in the Caribbean. The Taíno introduced them to squash, sweet potatoes, yams, and peanuts. Spanish settlers learned to use them in their food. They sent the foods back to Spain and introduced these new vegetables to Europe.

SPRING DWELLERS

+ **Manatees and alligators**

Ponce de León Springs lies inland from Daytona Beach, Florida. The explorer is believed to have visited this natural spring. The spring is home to **manatees** and alligators. Both animals were new to Ponce de León and his crew.

Fortune Hunting

The Spanish were eager to find gold in the Caribbean. Instead, Ponce de León made most of his money from farming. By 1513, he was wealthy enough to finance his first expedition to Florida.

EXPANDING EMPIRE

- Spanish monarchs eager to explore
- Official and unofficial expeditions

King Ferdinand and Queen Isabella hoped to expand the Spanish **empire** in the New World. They were eager to find out how many riches were there. Ponce de León made his expeditions on behalf of the crown. Other explorers did not follow the rules. It is quite possible that other Spanish adventurers may actually have reached Florida before him.

ROYAL FAVOR

- ★ Crown rewards explorer
- ★ Titles and riches bestowed

Ponce de León had proven his worth as governor of Higüey. In 1509, King Ferdinand made the explorer governor of San Juan Bautista (Puerto Rico). After claiming Florida for Spain, Ponce de León traveled back to Spain. In 1514, the king granted him rights to govern and colonize Florida.

SPREADING THE WORD

- ☞ Converting the Taíno
- ☞ Wealth counted in human souls

King Ferdinand and Queen Isabella believed strongly in their Christian religion. Europeans thought native peoples were "godless." The Spanish tried to convert them to Christianity. They forced the sons of Taíno chiefs to live with Spanish **missionaries**, who trained them as priests.

MAGIC FOUNTAIN

- ★ Explorers loved fame and honor
- ★ Sagas tell of great feats

It's possible that Ponce de León may have heard stories from the Taíno about a fountain whose waters provided eternal youth. However, many historians do not believe he did. Nevertheless, a park in St. Augustine, Florida, celebrates the story today. Founded in 1565, St. Augustine, was the capital of Spanish Florida for 200 years.

Did you know?

St. Augustine, the old Spanish capital of Florida, has been occupied for over 450 years. It is the longest continually inhabited European settlement in the United States.

I WANT TO BE RICH!

- + Island promises wealth for Ponce de León

San Juan Bautista was called Borikén by the Taíno. Ponce de León heard tales from the Taíno that the island was rich in gold. When he became governor, Ponce de León had the Taíno mine it for gold. The deposits were disappointing. By the mid-1500s, the Spanish had found silver in Mexico and South America.

This Isn't What It Said in the Brochure!

Ponce de León had a promising start to his career in Spain. However, setbacks and disappointments—and ultimately his death—awaited him in the New World.

Soldier

It was not unusual for men such as Ponce de León to face danger. After all, he was a soldier. At the time, violent clashes between enemies were relatively common.

REBELLION

- ☛ Taíno rebel
- ☛ Soldier called to act

Ponce de León twice faced rebellion by the Taíno. In 1504, he led attacks on the Taíno in Hispaniola to halt a revolt. When the Taíno in Puerto Rico rebelled in 1511, the Spanish fought back. This time, Agüeybaná, a chief who had befriended Ponce de León, died in the conflict. The relationship between the Spanish and the Taíno worsened.

SHORT-SIGHTED CHOICE

★ First Puerto Rico colony fails

The site Ponce de León chose in 1508 for his colony at Caparra in Puerto Rico was a poor one. The land was swampy and the colonists got sick. Ponce de León had to give up and move to a new location. The Taíno suffered greatly as the Spaniards made them build a series of forts and other buildings.

ACCESS DENIED

Ponce de León hoped to claim Bimini for Spain and himself. The Taíno had welcomed him, and he expected the same treatment elsewhere. This was not to be. As the Spanish expedition explored Florida's coastline in 1513, dozens of Calusa in canoes surrounded the ships. They yanked anchors and ropes away from the Spanish vessels. The Spanish retreated and did not return until 1521.

My Explorer Journal

★ Ponce de León was angry that Diego Columbus took his place as governor. Imagine you are Ponce. Write a letter to the King and Queen of Spain to explain why you should remain governor.

UNWELCOME VISITORS

☛ Calusa launched attack on Spanish colonists

☛ Leader fatally wounded

In June or July 1521, the Spaniards returned to Florida. The Calusa attacked, killing and wounding many soldiers, including Ponce de León. The crew took him to Cuba, but when they reached Havana, Ponce de León's wound became infected. He died in July 1521.

End of the Road

After Ponce de León, the Spanish wave of exploration continued into Mexico and South America. But no Europeans returned to Florida for another 40 years.

FLORIDA ABANDONED

☞ Spanish stayed clear

☞ Return to found missions

After Ponce de León's death, the Spanish did not attempt to settle Florida again until 1565. They founded St. Augustine and other missions. In the 1600s, the Spanish founded Pensacola. From 1763 to 1784, the British ruled Florida. In 1821, Florida became part of the new United States of America.

ONWARD TO MEXICO

★ Search for gold continues

Rather than settle Florida, Spanish explorers headed west to make new discoveries. In 1519, Spanish soldier Hernán Cortés led an expedition to Mexico, where he conquered the Aztec people and became governor of New Spain.

SPANISH AMERICA

+ **Language lives on**

+ **Spanish influence today**

Today, the Taíno influence can still be seen in English words, such as *hammock* and *maracas*. However, modern Puerto Ricans speak Spanish and follow the Catholic religion. The same is true of people in Cuba and the Dominican Republic.

GULF STREAM

★ **Ponce de León's discovery aids Spanish trade**

★ **Route used by many sailors**

Ponce de León's pilot, Anton de Alaminós, was the first sailor to take advantage of the Gulf Stream. He used it to return to Spain in 1519. After learning of this quick route home, other Spanish sailors also used it. American statesman Benjamin Franklin mapped the Gulf Stream in 1786.

HONORING THE MAN

☞ **Memorial to Ponce de León**

☞ **A fitting tribute**

In 1909, Ponce de León's remains were transported to San Juan Cathedral in the city named for him: Ponce, Puerto Rico. Today, the official language of Puerto Rico is still Spanish and the official religion is Catholicism—both legacies from exploration by Ponce de León.

Did you know?

There are many memorials to Ponce de León in Puerto Rico. One of the main streets in the capital, San Juan, is named for him. The island's second-largest city is also named Ponce.

GLOSSARY

archaeologists People who study the cultures of the distant past

arquebuses Early kinds of guns

caravel A small, fast type of sailing ship

colony A settlement or territory that is under the political control of a different country

compass A device used for navigation with a needle that always points to the north

cross-staff A tool for measuring angles between the horizon and the sun or the stars for purpose of navigation

dead reckoning Navigating by measuring one's speed and direction and the time of travel

empire A number of territories that all have the same ruler

encomienda A land system by which Spanish settlers demanded labor from native peoples

equator An imaginary line that runs around the middle of Earth

governor Someone who governs a place on behalf of a monarch

latitude A measure of how far a location is north or south of the equator

magnetized Describes a piece of metal that has been given magnetic qualities

manatees Water mammals, sometimes called sea cows

middens Piles of ancient food waste, particularly shells and bones

missionaries People who try to spread a religion, especially in a foreign land

Muslims People who observe the Islamic religion

New World A name for the Americas

page A young man being trained as a knight

pilot A sailor who is skilled at navigating in a particular area of water

quadrant An instrument used to measure the height of astronomical bodies above the horizon

scurvy A disease caused by lack of vitamin C

squire A knight's attendant

yucca A plant which is grown for food

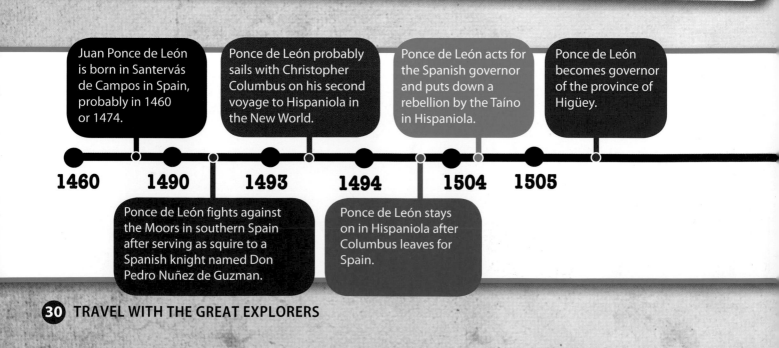

Juan Ponce de León is born in Santervás de Campos in Spain, probably in 1460 or 1474.

Ponce de León probably sails with Christopher Columbus on his second voyage to Hispaniola in the New World.

Ponce de León acts for the Spanish governor and puts down a rebellion by the Taíno in Hispaniola.

Ponce de León becomes governor of the province of Higüey.

1460   **1490**   **1493**   **1494**   **1504**   **1505**

Ponce de León fights against the Moors in southern Spain after serving as squire to a Spanish knight named Don Pedro Nuñez de Guzman.

Ponce de León stays on in Hispaniola after Columbus leaves for Spain.

ON THE WEB

latinamericanhistory.about.com/ od/latinamericatheconquest/p/ Biography-Of-Juan-Ponce-De-Leon. htm
Biography of Ponce de León.

fcit.usf.edu/florida/lessons/de_leon/ de_leon1.htm
Information about Ponce de León from the University of Southern Florida.

www.history.com/topics/exploration/ juan-ponce-de-leon
Links to videos about the explorer.

ageofex.marinersmuseum.org/index. php?type=explorer&id=66
A site by the Mariners' Museum with detailed information about Ponce de León and his discoveries.

BOOKS

Eagen, Rachel. *Juan Ponce de León: Exploring Florida and Puerto Rico* (In the Footsteps of Explorers). Crabtree, 2005.

Hoogenboom, Lynn. *Juan Ponce de León; A Primary Source Biography* (Primary Source Library of Famous Explorers). PowerKids Press, 2006.

Pelleschi, Andrea. *Juan Ponce de León* (Junior Graphic Famous Explorers). PowerKids Press, 2013.

Petrie, Kirsten. *Juan Ponce de León* (Explorers). Checkerboard Library, 2007.

Sutcliffe, Jane. *Juan Ponce de León* (History Maker Biographies). Lerner Publications, 2005.

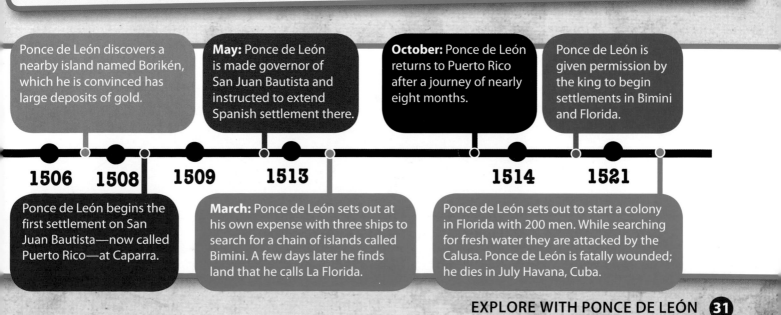

Ponce de León discovers a nearby island named Borikén, which he is convinced has large deposits of gold.

May: Ponce de León is made governor of San Juan Bautista and instructed to extend Spanish settlement there.

October: Ponce de León returns to Puerto Rico after a journey of nearly eight months.

Ponce de León is given permission by the king to begin settlements in Bimini and Florida.

1506   1508   1509   1513   1514   1521

Ponce de León begins the first settlement on San Juan Bautista—now called Puerto Rico—at Caparra.

March: Ponce de León sets out at his own expense with three ships to search for a chain of islands called Bimini. A few days later he finds land that he calls La Florida.

Ponce de León sets out to start a colony in Florida with 200 men. While searching for fresh water they are attacked by the Calusa. Ponce de León is fatally wounded; he dies in July Havana, Cuba.

INDEX